Faustina Logan.
Kilronan. from Santy.

Wizard of Oz

Illustrated by Eric Kincaid

RED
CIRCLE

Dorothy lived with her Aunt Em and Uncle Henry. She had a small dog called Toto.

One day there was a whirlwind. Dorothy and Toto were alone in the house. The whirlwind lifted them up high into the sky.

The house came to rest in the
Land of the Munchkins. It fell
on top of the Wicked Witch of
the East and killed her.
The Munchkins were very pleased.
They gave Dorothy the Wicked
Witch of the East's magic shoes.

"Can you help me find my way home?" she asked the Munchkins. They shook their heads. They did not know the way.
"Go to the Emerald City," they said. "Ask the Wizard of Oz to help you." Dorothy put on the magic shoes and set off along the yellow brick road with Toto.

After many miles
Dorothy met
a Scarecrow.
"Can I go to the
Emerald City with
you?" said the
Scarecrow. "Perhaps
the Wizard of Oz
will give me
a brain."

The next day they
found a Tin Man
in the forest.
"Can I go with
you?" said the Tin
Man. "Perhaps the
Wizard of Oz will
give me a heart."

A Lion jumped out of the bushes
and roared. It tried to bite Toto.
Dorothy slapped the Lion.
"How dare you bite a little dog!
You are a coward!" said Dorothy.
"I know," said the Lion. "But how
can I help it? Do you think the
Wizard of Oz would give me some
courage?"

They went across ditches and over rivers. At last they came to the Land of Oz. They went to the Emerald City. Everything in the city was green.

The Wizard of Oz lived in a palace. He was a magician. He could change the way he looked.

In the Throne Room all Dorothy
could see was a huge green head.
"I am Oz," said a voice. "Who
are you and why do you seek me?"
Dorothy told him she wanted
to find the way home.
"I will help if you kill the
Wicked Witch of the West," said
the Wizard.

The Scarecrow saw
the Wizard as
a green lady.

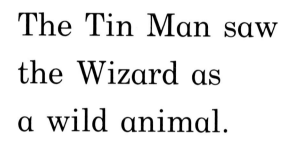

The Tin Man saw
the Wizard as
a wild animal.

The Lion saw him
as a ball of fire.

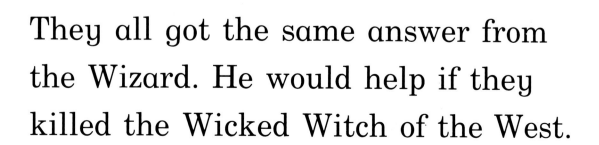

They all got the same answer from
the Wizard. He would help if they
killed the Wicked Witch of the West.

The Wicked Witch of the West
saw them coming. She tried to stop
them.

The Tin Man killed the wolves.
The Scarecrow caught the crows.
The bees broke their stings when
they tried to sting the Tin Man.
The Winkies ran away when the
Lion roared.

The Wicked Witch of the West was
angry. She sent the fierce Flying
Monkeys after them. They dropped
the Tin Man on to some rocks.
He broke into pieces. They pulled
the straw out of the Scarecrow.
They put the Lion into a cage.

The Flying Monkeys took Dorothy
and Toto to the Wicked Witch's
castle. The Witch saw Dorothy's
magic shoes and began to shake.
The Wicked Witch kicked Toto.
That made Dorothy very angry.

She picked up a bucket of water
and threw it over the Witch.
Then as Dorothy looked on in
wonder, the Witch began to shrink
and fall away. Then there was
nothing but a puddle. The Wicked
Witch of the West was dead.

Dorothy let the Lion out of the cage. The Winkies helped her put the straw back into the Scarecrow. They helped her put the Tin Man back together.

When they returned to the palace
the Throne Room was empty. The
Lion gave a roar and knocked over
a screen. Hiding behind it was
a little man. It was the Wizard.
"I am not really a wizard," he said.
"People only think I am because I
can do tricks. But I will help you
if I can."

The Wizard filled
the Scarecrow's
head with sharp
things like pins
and needles.
"Now you have
a brain," he said.

He took a red silk
heart stuffed with
sawdust and put it
inside the Tin Man.

He gave the Lion
a drink that would
give him courage.

He made a balloon so that Dorothy
and Toto could fly home. The
balloon took off before Dorothy was
ready. It flew away without her.

The Good Witch of the South came
to rescue Dorothy.
"Tap your heels together three
times and tell the magic shoes
where you want to go," she said.

The Good Witch of the South made
the Scarecrow ruler of the Emerald
City. She made the Tin Man ruler
of the Winkies. She made the Lion
King of the Forest.
Dorothy and Toto went home
to Aunt Em and Uncle Henry.

All these appear in the pages of
the story. Can you find them?

Dorothy and Toto

Scarecrow

Tin Man

Wicked Witch